My First Animal Kingdom Encyclopedias

# BIRDS

by Pamela Dell

Consultant:
Jackie Gai, DVM
Wildlife Veterinarian

CAPSTONE PRESS
a capstone imprint

A+ Books are published by Capstone Press,
1710 Roe Crest Drive, North Mankato, Minnesota 56003
www.mycapstone.com

Library of Congress Cataloging-in-Publication data is available on the Library of
Congress website.
ISBN 978-1-5157-3927-2 (library binding)
ISBN 978-1-5157-3938-8 (paperback)
ISBN 978-1-5157-3967-8 (eBook PDF)

Summary: A photo-illustrated reference guide to birds that highlights physical features,
diet, life cycles, and more.

**Editorial Credits**
Kathryn Clay, editor; Rick Korab and Juliette Peters, designers;
Kelly Garvin, media researcher; Gene Bentdahl, production specialist

**Photo Credits**
Minden Pictures: Andrew M. Snyder/NIS, 9 (bottom right), Filippo Nucifora, 9 (bottom left),
Martin Withers/FLPA, 13 (top), Robert Royse/BIA, 17 (top right), Tui De Roy, 25 (top left);
Shutterstock: aaltair, 16 (bottom), Andrea Izzotti, 8 (tr), 25 (br), Ana Gram, 18 (middle), Anneka,
13 (m), AuntSpray, 24 (t), BOONCHUAY PROMJIAM, cover (br), Borislav Borisov, 4 (b), Brian
Lasenby, 15 (br), ChameleonsEye, 11 (b), Chris Humphries, 10 (br), Connie Barr, 29 (tr), Dima
Fadeev, 10 (t), Dmytro Pylypenko, 8 (br), duangnapa_b, 8 (left), Ellen Koppen-Fodeilanal, 21
(middle right), Eric Isselee, cover (tr), 9 (tl), Ethan Daniels, 17 (m), Evgeny SHCH, cover (bl),
FlordiaStock, 26 (m), FotoRequest, 14 (b), francesco de marco, 30 (bl), Galina Savina, 9 (tr),
GUDKOV ANDREY, 10 (bl), 15 (m), hin255, 24 (b), Igor Kovalenko, 18 (t), Jeff Hackett, 20-21,
JeremyRichards, 32, Jessie Nguyen 15 (tr), John Carnemolla, 30 (br), jurra8, 27 (t), Karel Gallas,
13 (b), Karen Givens, 17 (tl), Kemeo, 16 (bottom middle), Keneva Photography, 27 (m), Kichigin,
8-9, Kotomiti Okuma, 1 (right), Krivosheev Vitaly, cover, 1 (bkg), leungchopan, 28 (b), Lucie
Vonaskova, 6-7, Marcus VDT, 22-23, 31 (tl), Marcos Amend, 23 (t), Maria Gaellman, 11 (ml),
Mark Medical, 26-27, Martin Mecnarowski, 28-29, Mauricio S. Ferreira, 17 (b), Mauro Rodrigues,
21 (t), Menno Schaefer, 14 (t), Mirko Rosenau, 30 (tl), Natural Earth Imagery, 24-25, Oldrich,
16 (t), Ondrej Prosicky, 14-15, 15 (bl), paula french, 25 (tr), Phil Lowe, 29 (tl), Photoinjection,
18 (b), rck_953, 19 (t), Robin Keefe, 20 (b), Roger Clark ARPS, 12 (b), Sanit Fuangnakhon, 4-5,
scooperdigital, 11, (t), Sebastian Knight, 5 (b), Serg Zastakin, 16-17, Sergej Razvodovskij, 20 (t),
sichkarenko.com, 21 (b), silentwings, 21 (ml), sharftinaction, 1 (l), Stefan Holm, 19 (bm), Steve
Byland, back cover, 29 (br), StevensRussellSmithPhotos, 19 (b), Sue Robinson, 30 (tr), Sunny
Forest, 18-19, Super Prin, 15 (tl), 23 (m) (b), The Len, 31 (bl), titov dmitriy, 20 (m), tjwvandongen,
31 (br), Tobie Oosthuizen, cover (tl), Tony Brindley, 19 (tm), Tory Kallman 25 (bl), Tracy Starr, 11
(mr), Vitaly Titov, 12-13, Vladimir Kogan Michael, 27 (b), Warren Price Photography,
29 (bl), Wendy Rentz, 12 (t), Wendy Townrow, 31 (tr), wolfman57, 10-11, Zocchi Roberto,
16 (tm), Zubada, 2-3

Artistic Elements: Shutterstock: Fotonium, Krivosheev Vitaly, Panu Ruangjan, Zubada

Printed in the United States of America.
10025817

# TABLE OF CONTENTS

# What Are Birds?

Birds are animals with wings, feathers, and a beak. They are egg-laying animals. Most birds can fly.

**class**
a smaller group of living things; birds are in the class Aves (AY-veez)

**phylum**
(FIE-lum)
a group of living things with a similar body plan; birds belong to the phylum Chordata (kawr-DEY-tuh); mammals, reptiles, and fish are also in this group

**order**
a group of living things that is smaller than a class; there are 23 orders of birds

**kingdom**
one of five very large groups into which all living things are placed; the two main kingdoms are plants and animals; birds belong to the animal kingdom

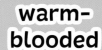

**warm-blooded**
having a body temperature that stays about the same all the time, no matter the surroundings; birds and mammals are warm-blooded

**vertebrate**
(VUR-tuh-brit)
an animal that has a backbone; birds are vertebrates

**passerines**
(PASS-er-inz)
the largest order of birds; more than half of all birds are passerines; all passerines have feet made for perching

**species**
(SPEE-sees)
a group of animals that are alike and can produce young with each other; there are about 10,000 species of birds

# Part by Part

Birds come in all sizes. But they share many of the same body parts.

**nape**
the back of a bird's neck

**throat**
the front of a bird's neck

**wattle**
a fleshy flap of skin that hangs from the neck of some birds; chicken wattles are usually bright red

**breast**
the part of a bird's body just below the throat

**crown**
the top
of a bird's
head

**beak**
a bird's
hard, usually
pointed mouthpart;
sometimes called
a bill

**field
marks**
the colors, spots,
and lines on a bird's
body that help
tell one species
from another

**wing**
a body
part used for
flying or gliding;
birds have two
wings

# Feathered Friends

Birds are the only animals with feathers. Their feathers help them fly and keep warm. Colorful feathers may even help birds find mates.

**down**
short, fluffy feathers; newly hatched chicks are covered with down

**tail feathers**
feathers that stick out from the end of a bird's body; these feathers help birds turn and stop when flying

**molt**
to shed old feathers so new ones can grow; ptarmigans molt twice a year; their feathers are white in winter and brown in summer

## eyering

(I-ring): a narrow ring of feathers that circles a bird's eye; eyerings are different in color from a bird's body

## train

the long tail feathers that some male birds have; the peacock lifts his flashy train and shakes it to attract females

## ruff

a ring of feathers circling a bird's neck; male sandpipers have a puffy ruff

## crest

a group of feathers that grows from the top of a bird's head; northern royal flycatchers have a large, spotted crest in orange, red, or yellow

# What Birds Do

**crow**
to make
a loud call;
roosters
crow

**hover**
(HUH-ver)
to float in the air
using wind currents or
wing movements; kestrels
hover while watching for
mice below; then they
swoop down to
make a kill

**dance**
some birds
do a fancy dance
to attract mates;
flamingoes dance
in large groups

**preen**
to clean
and straighten
feathers; preening
also helps remove
bugs and dust from
the feathers

**stoop**
the fast,
steep dive
of a bird of
prey

**mimic**
(MIM-ick)
to look or sound
like something else;
some parrots can
learn to mimic
human voices

**roost**
to settle down
for a night's rest;
birds do not roost
in the nests they build
for egg-laying; many
birds roost in trees
or bushes

**swim**
penguins
cannot fly, but
they are fast
swimmers

# Raising a Family

Birds work hard to survive. Many birds form pairs to make their work easier. These parent birds build nests for the eggs that the mother bird will lay.

**nest**
a structure built by animals to hold their eggs; bird nests are usually made of sticks, leaves, and mud; they're often lined with grass, feathers, or spider silk

**egg**
birds lay eggs with hard shells; shell colors vary by species

**clutch**
a group of eggs that are all laid around the same time

**incubate**
(IN-kyoo-bate): to warm eggs by sitting on them so the chicks inside will hatch; male emperor penguins incubate their mate's egg for more than two months

**brood patch**
an area of bare skin on a bird's belly used to cover and keep eggs warm

## hatch
to break out of an egg

## chick
a newly hatched bird

## egg tooth
a sharp bump at the end of a chick's beak; the egg tooth helps the chick break out of the egg; after the chick hatches, its egg tooth disappears

## brood
a family of young birds that hatch at about the same time

## nestling
a young bird that's not old enough to leave the nest

## regurgitate
(ri-GUR-ji-tayt): to spit up food that has already been swallowed; many birds regurgitate their food to feed their young

# What's for Dinner?

Some birds eat plants. Others eat animals. Let's see what's on the menu.

## food chain
a series of living things in which each one eats the one before it; golden eagles are at the top of their food chain

## predator
(PRED-uh-tur) an animal that hunts other animals for food

## prey
(PRAY): an animal hunted by another animal for food; mice, smaller birds, and rabbits are common prey for hawks

## carnivore
(KAHR-nuh-vor): an animal that eats only meat; birds of prey, such as eagles and owls, are carnivores

## seeds
seeds are a common food source for birds; blue jays eat sunflower seeds

**nectar**
(NEK-ter)
a sweet liquid found in flowers; hummingbirds use tube-like tongues to collect and drink nectar

**insects**
small animals with sectioned bodies and six legs; ants, beetles, and other insects are one of the most common foods for wild birds

**carrion**
(KAR-ee-uhn)
the bodies of dead animals; vultures eat carrion

**fish**
pelicans swoop into the water to catch fish in their large throat pouches; other birds spear fish with their pointed beaks

**brine shrimp**
tiny shrimp that live in salty lakes and seas; flamingoes get their pink color from eating brine shrimp

# Nothing but Nests

Some bird nests are big and messy. Others are as small as a walnut! But all birds make nests for the same reason. They want a safe place for their young to hatch and grow.

**cupped nest**
a nest shaped like a cup; made of many different materials and found in trees or bushes

**ground nest**
usually a cupped nest built right on the ground; swans build ground nests

**mud nest**
a nest built of mud and sometimes animal droppings; the sun dries the mud into hard clay

**hanging nest**
a long, sack-like nest that hangs from a tree or place above the ground; orioles build hanging nests

### cliff nest
a nest built on a high, rocky ledge; puffins build cliff nests

### scrape nest
a type of ground nest made by making a shallow hole; killdeer build scrape nests

### saliva nest
a nest made completely out of spit, or saliva; Asian swiftlets use their saliva to build nests on the sides of cliffs

### cavity nest
a nest made in a tree hole or other empty space; hornbills make cavity nests inside hollow trees

### burrow
a tunnel or hole in the ground made or used by an animal; burrowing owls find holes that rabbits or other animals have already dug

# On the Move

When the days turn cold, plants die off. Food is hard to find. Many birds fly to warmer parts of the world to find enough to eat. They return when the warm weather returns.

## migrate

(MYE-grate): to move from one place to another when seasons change in order to find food or to mate; some birds may fly thousands of miles to reach their new homes

## V-formation

(VEE for-MAY-shun): the V-shaped pattern that migrating geese take when they fly together; the shape helps the geese save energy and stay together; birds take turns flying at the front

## navigate

(NAV-ih-gate): to find the way over a long distance; scientists do not fully understand how birds navigate to their winter homes every year

## Canada goose

a common North American migrating bird; Canada geese fly north in spring and south in fall

## flyway

a route taken every year by large groups of migrating birds; North America has four flyways: the Pacific, the Atlantic, the Central, and the Mississippi

## fallout

the landing of large groups of birds when they are in trouble during migration; a fallout happens mainly when the birds are too tired, weak, and hungry to fly any longer

## route

(ROWT): a path taken to get from one place to another; many migrating birds, such as cranes, follow the same route year after year

## resident

(REZ-uh-dent): a bird that does not migrate; resident birds can live in cold places as long as they have enough food; chickadees are resident birds

# Water Birds

Many birds live in and around water. They dive, glide, and fish for food.

**waterfowl**
large water birds with rounded bills and webbed feet; swans are waterfowl; so are ducks and geese

**duckling**
a baby duck

**webbed feet**
feet with toes that are joined together by a flap of skin; webbed feet help water birds swim and dive

**waterproof**
able to keep water out; the feathers of water birds are waterproof

## wetlands

land that is full of water and water plants; birds such as egrets hide, hunt for food, and nest in wetlands

## drake

a male duck; mallard drakes have bright green heads to set them apart from females (brown heads)

## shorebird

also called a wader; a bird that spends most of its time around water; storks nest on the shore and wade into the water to catch food

## pelagic

(pel-AH-jik) animals that live on or in the open ocean and far from shore; pelagic birds, such as pelicans, come to land only to lay eggs and raise young

## precocial

(pree-COH-shul) born already having feathers and open eyes; unlike other birds, water birds are precocial

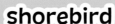

# Tropical Birds

Tropical birds live in hot parts of the world. They are known for their bright, colorful feathers.

**rain forest**
a thick area of trees where rain falls almost every day; many tropical birds live in the rain forests of South America

**toucan**
(TOO-kan)
a brightly colored tropical bird; toucans have short legs and a long, colorful beak

**equator**
(ih-KWAY-tur)
the imaginary line that circles Earth and divides the northern half from the southern half

**Amazon Basin**
the area of land in South America where the waters of the Amazon River drain; more than 1,500 bird species live in this area

**tropical**
having to
do with the hot,
humid part of the
world near the
equator called
the tropics

**canopy**
(KAN-uh-pee)
the treetops of the
highest trees in a
rain forest; hoatzins
live in the rain
forest canopy

**plumage**
(PLOO-mij)
another name for
a bird's feathers;
scarlet macaws have
bright red, blue, and
gold plumage

**parrot**
a brightly
colored tropical
bird with a large
beak; two of the
largest parrot species
are macaws and
cockatoos

**macaws**

23

# Flightless Birds

Most birds can fly. But about 40 species cannot. Birds that cannot fly often have a hard time escaping predators. Some species have died out.

**elephant bird**
an extinct bird that lived on only one island east of Africa; the elephant bird was the largest bird that ever lived; it weighed almost as much as a grizzly bear

**extinct**
(ek-STINGKT)
no longer living; an extinct animal is one that has died out, with no more of its kind on Earth; dodo birds (like the pictured models) likely became extinct in the late 1600s

**ratites**
(RA-tites)
a large group of birds that have no muscles to fly; ostriches are ratites

**penguin**
a type of flightless water bird; penguins have webbed feet and use their wings as flippers

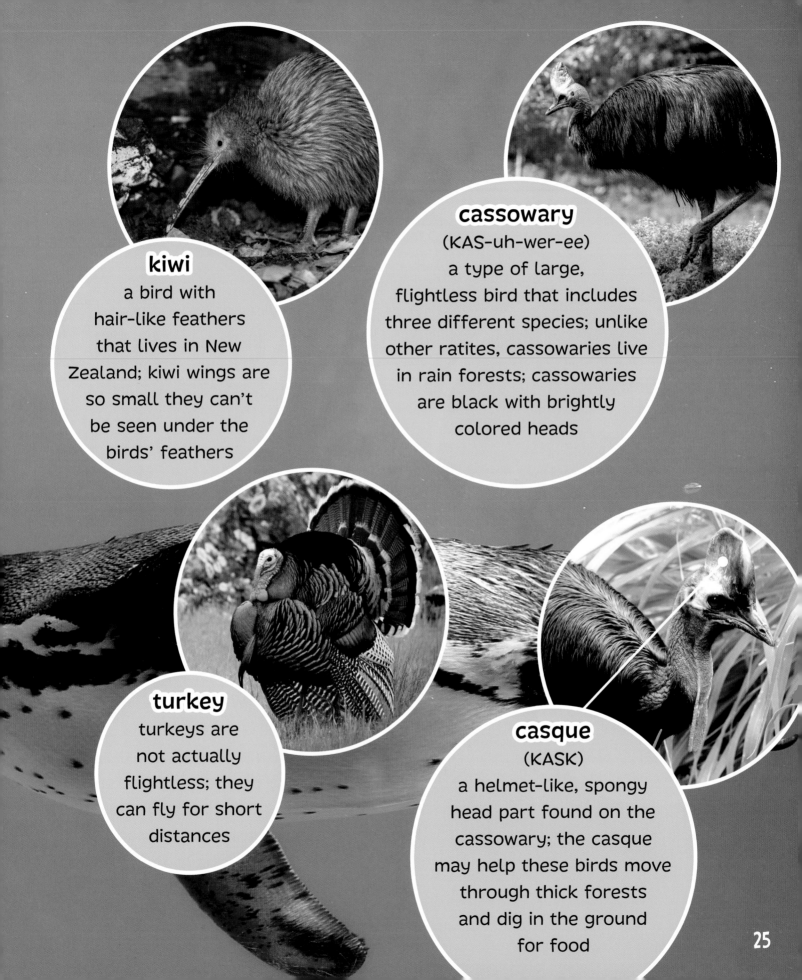

## kiwi
a bird with hair-like feathers that lives in New Zealand; kiwi wings are so small they can't be seen under the birds' feathers

## cassowary
(KAS-uh-wer-ee)
a type of large, flightless bird that includes three different species; unlike other ratites, cassowaries live in rain forests; cassowaries are black with brightly colored heads

## turkey
turkeys are not actually flightless; they can fly for short distances

## casque
(KASK)
a helmet-like, spongy head part found on the cassowary; the casque may help these birds move through thick forests and dig in the ground for food

# Birds of Prey

Their eyesight is sharp. So are their hooked beaks and claws. Birds of prey are fierce hunters.

**solitary**
(SOL-ih-tayr-ee)
alone; most raptors live alone or in very small groups

**raptor**
another name for a bird of prey; raptors include owls, eagles, and vultures; there are nearly 450 raptor species

**wingspan**
the measure of a bird's wings from the tip of one wing to the tip of the other; female raptors have longer wingspans than male raptors

**nocturnal**
(nok-TUR-nuhl)
active at night;
most owls rest
during the day and
hunt at night

**owls**
raptors
with big eyes and
round heads; special
feathers allow owls to
fly without making
any sound

**falcon**

**hawks**
the group
name for raptors
that includes
eagles, falcons,
kites, and
osprey

**talon**
a sharp claw
on a bird of
prey; an osprey's
talons are curved
to catch fish

# Bird-watching

Some birds make good pets. Others are fun to watch from a distance. Seeing birds fly can give people a feeling of freedom. Their beautiful songs bring people joy.

**binoculars**
(buh-NOK-yuh-lerz)
a tool for seeing faraway things up close; bird-watchers use binoculars to study birds they can't get close to

**hobby**
an activity done for fun; bird-watching is a hobby many people enjoy

**dawn chorus**
(DAWN KOR-us)
a group of many different birds all singing together just before the sun comes up; scientists aren't sure why birds sing at dawn and then go quiet

## birdhouse

a house made by people for birds to nest in; bluebirds like small, narrow houses with a little hole at the top

## songbird

a bird known for the special songlike calls it makes; almost half of all birds are songbirds

## warble

to sing softly in sounds that keep changing; the yellow warbler has a high-pitched warbling song

## birdbath

a shallow dish for birds to bathe in; people often set up birdbaths in their yard or garden

# Fun Facts

A **group of geese** is called a gaggle.

The fastest bird in the world is the **peregrine falcon**. It can dive-bomb faster than 200 miles (322 kilometers) per hour.

When **puffins** fly, their wings flap about 400 times per minute.

**Ostriches** reach running speeds of up to 45 miles (72 km) per hour.

The **harpy eagle** lives in the rain forests of Central and South America. To help catch prey, its claws can grow as large as a grizzly bear's.

The **southern cassowary** lives in Australia. It's known as the most dangerous bird in the world. When afraid, these birds go into attack mode. Sometimes they kill even large mammals like dogs.

**Chickens** are the closest living relatives to the Tyrannosaurus rex.

**Horned coots** build their own islands in shallow water. They gather pebbles together and drop them in one place in the water over and over until an island forms. Then they cover it with plants. They make their nests on the islands.

# READ MORE

**Calmenson, Stephanie**. *Look! Birds!* New York: Little Bee Books, an imprint of Bonnier Publishing Group, 2016.

**Martin, Isabel**. *Birds: A Question and Answer Book*. Animal Kingdom Questions and Answers. North Mankato, Minn.: Capstone Press, a Capstone imprint, 2015.

**Sill, Cathryn**. *About Birds: A Guide for Children. / Sobre los pájaros: Una guía para niños*. Atlanta: Peachtree Publishers, 2014.

# INTERNET SITES

FactHound offers a safe, fun way to find Internet sites related to this book. All of the sites on FactHound have been researched by our staff.

Here's all you do:
Visit *www.facthound.com*
Type in this code:
9781515739272

Super-cool stuff! Check out projects, games and lots more at **www.capstonekids.com**